HUMAN BODY SYSTEMS

The Human
Circulatory System

By Cassie M. Lawton

New York

Published in 2021 by Cavendish Square Publishing, LLC
243 5th Avenue, Suite 136, New York, NY 10016

Website: cavendishsq.com

This publication represents the opinions and views of the author based on his or her personal experience, knowledge, and research. The information in this book serves as a general guide only. The author and publisher have used their best efforts in preparing this book and disclaim liability rising directly or indirectly from the use and application of this book.

Portions of this work were originally authored by Autumn Leigh and published as *The Circulatory System (The Human Body)*. All new material this edition authored by Cassie M. Lawton.

All websites were available and accurate when this book was sent to press.

Library of Congress Cataloging-in-Publication Data

Names: Lawton, Cassie M., author.
Title: The human circulatory system / Cassie M. Lawton.
Description: First edition. | New York : Cavendish Square Publishing, 2021.
| Series: The inside guide: human body systems | Includes bibliographical references and index.
Identifiers: LCCN 2019049697 (print) | LCCN 2019049698 (ebook) |
ISBN 9781502657190 (library binding) | ISBN 9781502657176 (paperback) |
ISBN 9781502657183 (set) | ISBN 9781502657206 (ebook)
Subjects: LCSH: Cardiovascular system–Juvenile literature. |
CYAC: Circulatory system.
Classification: LCC QP103 .L39 2021 (print) | LCC QP103 (ebook) |
DDC 612.1–dc23
LC record available at https://lccn.loc.gov/2019049697
LC ebook record available at https://lccn.loc.gov/2019049698

Editor: Kristen Susienka
Copy Editor: Nathan Heidelberger
Designer: Deanna Paternostro

Some of the images in this book illustrate individuals who are models. The depictions do not imply actual situations or events.

CPSIA compliance information: Batch #CS20CSQ: For further information contact Cavendish Square Publishing LLC, New York, New York, at 1-877-980-4450.

Printed in the United States of America

CONTENTS

The circulatory system carries blood throughout the body.

ALL FOR THE HEART

The human body is like a complex highway. Inside, there are many different pathways, or systems, working to spread important materials to every part. Sometimes, this is information; other times, it's oxygen or blood. Without these systems, it would be impossible to live. One of the most important pathways is the circulatory system, which is also known as the cardiovascular system.

What Is It?

Blood is constantly circulating, or moving, throughout the human body, pushed through **blood vessels** by the pumping of the heart. Together, the blood, blood vessels, and heart make up the circulatory system. Without a circulatory system, our bodies wouldn't be able to function the way they do.

Fast Fact

Added up, all the blood vessels in a single human are about 60,000 miles (100,000 kilometers) long!

What Does It Do?

The circulatory system has two main jobs within the human body. First, it's responsible for transporting **nutrients**, water, oxygen, and chemicals to organs and tissues all over

OPEN SYSTEM VS. CLOSED SYSTEM

There are two types of circulatory systems: open and closed. Humans and many other large animals have a closed circulatory system. This means blood is pumped through a closed path of blood vessels. Nutrients in the blood pass through the walls of the tiniest blood vessels to reach organs, but the blood itself stays inside the blood vessels. Smaller creatures, such as insects and snails, have open circulatory systems. The blood in their bodies is pumped out of vessels and into spaces, called cavities, that contain organs. Nutrients pass directly from the blood into these organs.

An open circulatory system is simpler, but it would not make sense in a human or large animal. Since the blood is simply flushed onto the organs, open systems use less energy, but they aren't as good at getting oxygen to every part of the body. Many of the creatures with open systems don't need as much oxygen in their bodies, though, because they don't move around much. An open system works well for their needs. Humans and other animals with closed circulatory systems are more active. That means they need to move more oxygen through their bodies quicker. Therefore, a more complex system, like the closed system, is useful, as individual highways of blood vessels pump material to all parts of the body rapidly.

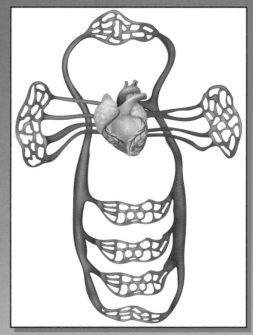

This is a simplified model of the human circulatory system, which is an example of a closed system.

our bodies. It delivers all the things a body needs to function properly. Second, it transports waste products, such as **carbon dioxide**, to locations where they can be eliminated, or removed, from the body.

What's the Heart Got to Do with It?

You might consider your heart the motor of your circulatory system. It makes sure blood is always moving through the blood vessels, even when you're asleep. This ensures that the circulatory system continuously supplies your cells and organs with fresh nutrients and oxygen while removing waste products.

Your heart is about the size of your fist. It's located in the middle of your chest, between your lungs and slightly to the left of the center of your body. The rib cage keeps it safe. The heart is made of a special kind of muscle called cardiac muscle. We don't have to think about moving our heart as we do muscles such as those in our arms and legs. The heart keeps moving on its own. Each movement is called a heartbeat, or beat for short.

When you put your hand up to your chest, you can feel your heart beating. What you're feeling is your heart expanding (getting bigger) and contracting (getting smaller) very quickly. This movement—your heartbeat—is what keeps your blood flowing. A single heartbeat lasts about 0.8 seconds. The average human heart beats about 75 times a minute, 100,000 times a day, and 40 million times a year. It can beat more than 3 billion times in a lifetime.

Fast Fact

A device called a pacemaker can help people with irregular, or unsteady, heartbeats. It's put in the human body and helps the heart muscle contract.

A fast heartbeat means the heart is working hard to pump blood through the body.

In one day, about 2,000 gallons (7,570 liters) of blood pass through the human heart. The heart needs oxygen to beat, and blood brings oxygen to the heart.

A Heart Divided

The human heart is a pump. Actually, it's two pumps. The heart has four divisions, or chambers, arranged on two sides. The upper and lower chambers on each side form a pump. Each upper chamber is called an atrium. Each lower, larger chamber is called a ventricle.

The atrium on the right side of the heart receives blood from the body. Blood passes from the atrium into the right ventricle and is pumped to the lungs. The left atrium receives blood from the lungs, and the left ventricle pumps it to the rest of the body. The left ventricle is the largest and strongest

Fast Fact

In the 4th century BCE, a Greek thinker named Aristotle said the human heart was the most important part of the body.

chamber of the heart. It needs to be strong to pump blood throughout the body. The left and right sides of the heart are separated by a wall of muscle called the septum. Altogether, these parts work to keep blood pumping continuously throughout the human body.

The heart has four valves that control blood flow. The tricuspid valve controls blood flow between the right atrium and right ventricle. The pulmonary valve allows blood to flow from the right ventricle out to the lungs to get oxygen. Oxygen-rich blood from the lungs passes from the left atrium into the left ventricle through the mitral valve. The aortic valve allows blood to pass from the left ventricle out to the rest of the body.

A healthy heart means oxygen is flowing. If someone's heart stops beating and they don't get help right away, they could die.

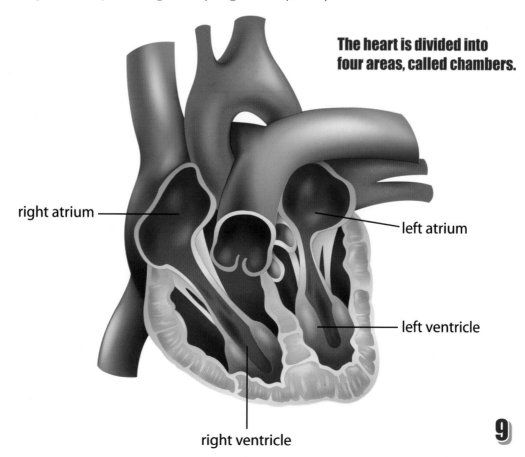

The heart is divided into four areas, called chambers.

right atrium

left atrium

left ventricle

right ventricle

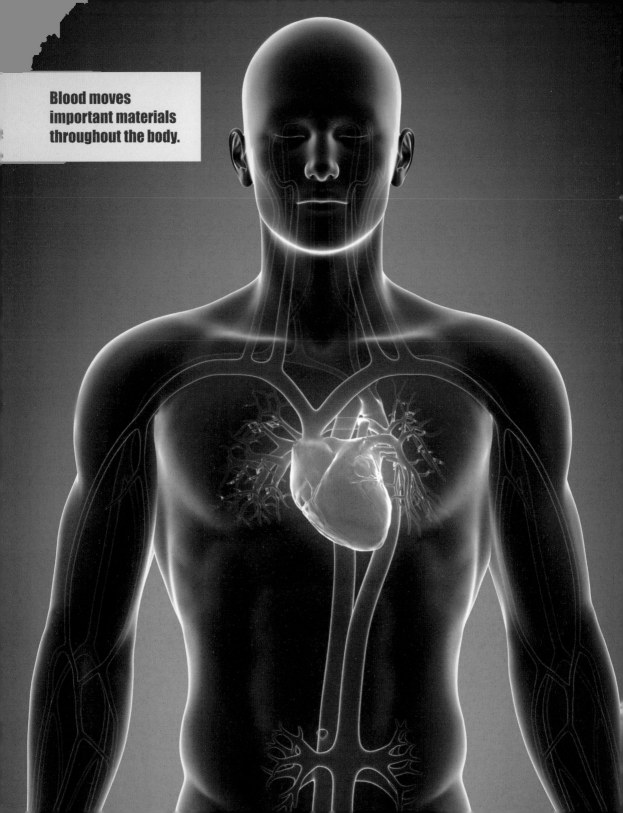

Blood moves important materials throughout the body.

Chapter Two

BLOOD VESSELS: THE HIGHWAY TO THE HEART

One of the main transporters of oxygen through the human body is blood. Blood is part of the circulatory highway. Blood vessels carry blood containing oxygen to **extremities**. All blood vessels depend on the heart. This is the main headquarters of the human body's circulatory system. There are three main kinds of blood vessels: arteries, capillaries, and veins. As they extend farther and farther from the heart, blood vessels branch out into increasingly smaller tubes.

Arteries

Arteries, the strongest of the blood vessels, carry blood away from the heart. Most arteries deliver oxygenated, or oxygen-rich, blood throughout the body. The aorta, which begins at the left ventricle, is the largest artery. It rises out of the top of the heart, turns downward, and extends just below the **diaphragm**. Carotid arteries travel up the neck and provide the brain with oxygenated blood. The femoral arteries are large blood vessels that run through the thighs. The coronary arteries bring oxygenated blood to the heart itself. The pulmonary arteries carry blood from the right ventricle of the heart to the lungs to

Fast Fact

The inside space of a blood vessel is called a lumen.

Arteries are the body's toughest blood vessels.

get oxygen. They're the only arteries that carry **deoxygenated** blood.

Veins

Veins carry oxygen-poor blood from the rest of the body back to the heart. They're thinner than arteries and not as strong. Since the veins carry the body's waste products, it's important that blood isn't allowed to flow backward in them. To stop this from happening, veins have tiny valves to keep blood flowing toward the heart.

Arteries and veins have three layers. The outside layer supports the blood vessel by connecting it to surrounding tissues. This holds the vessel in place. The middle layer is muscle, which works with the heart to keep blood flowing. It's usually the thickest layer. The inner layer is very thin. It's the layer that's in contact with the blood.

Fast Fact

The largest veins are the superior vena cava and inferior vena cava. They connect directly to the heart.

Capillaries

Capillaries connect the arteries to the veins. They're the

Blood is red, but veins look blue under our skin because of the way they reflect light back to our eyes.

UNDERSTANDING YOUR PULSE

Just like the heart, arteries expand and contract. Their movements are the result of the heart beating. You can feel your arteries moving by pressing your fingers on certain arteries, such as the carotid arteries in your neck or the radial arteries in your wrists. The movement you feel is called your pulse. Your pulse tells you how fast your heart is beating. It tells you about your heart's rhythm and strength.

Many people check their heart rate when exercising by checking their own pulse. A body's pulse is different depending on what the person is doing. If they're exercising, their pulse is likely fast. If they're resting or sleeping, their pulse most often will be slower. Sometimes, people who exercise a lot have a slower heart rate when sitting or lying down, compared to people who don't exercise much. A heart rate of below 60 heartbeats per minute is called bradycardia and is considered slower than average.

Exercising will get your pulse racing!

smallest of the blood vessels. Most are only one cell thick. Capillaries are so thin that oxygen and nutrients can pass through their walls and into the surrounding tissues. Carbon dioxide passes from the tissues into the capillaries.

Blood Vessel Type	Purpose and Features
artery	carries blood away from heart; thick walls; narrow lumen
vein	carries blood to the heart; thin walls; wide lumen; valves to stop blood flowing backward
capillary	brings nutrients to cells and takes waste products away from cells; very thin walls; very narrow lumen

Circulation Types

Two kinds of circulation occur within the circulatory system: pulmonary and systemic. Pulmonary circulation involves the movement of deoxygenated blood from the heart to the lungs and oxygenated blood from the lungs to the heart. Blood reaches the lungs through the pulmonary arteries. Capillaries in the lungs exchange carbon dioxide for oxygen, and the blood travels back to the heart through the pulmonary veins.

Systemic circulation involves the movement of oxygenated blood from the heart to the body and deoxygenated blood from the body back to the heart. Blood leaves the heart through the aorta, which branches out into increasingly smaller arteries. After passing through the capillaries and releasing

Fast Fact

The muscle layer in arteries is very strong to help keep blood pumping. The interior layer is very smooth. This allows blood to flow more quickly.

The lungs are shown here on the sides of the heart.

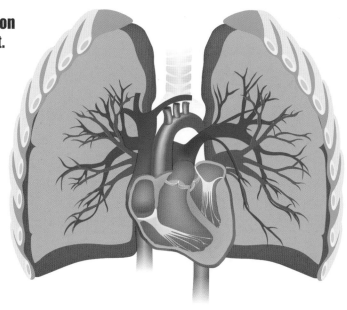

oxygen, the blood returns to the heart through the veins.

Another type of circulation involves the kidneys. It's called renal circulation. "Renal" means having to do with the kidneys. Renal circulation is a part of systemic circulation. Oxygen-rich blood enters the kidneys through the renal arteries. These arteries branch out into capillaries, which take the blood to the parts of the kidneys that filter out waste products. Waste products come from the natural breakdown of tissues and from food. The kidneys send the waste to the bladder in the form of urine. The "clean" blood then returns to the heart.

Kidneys flush out waste materials from our bodies.

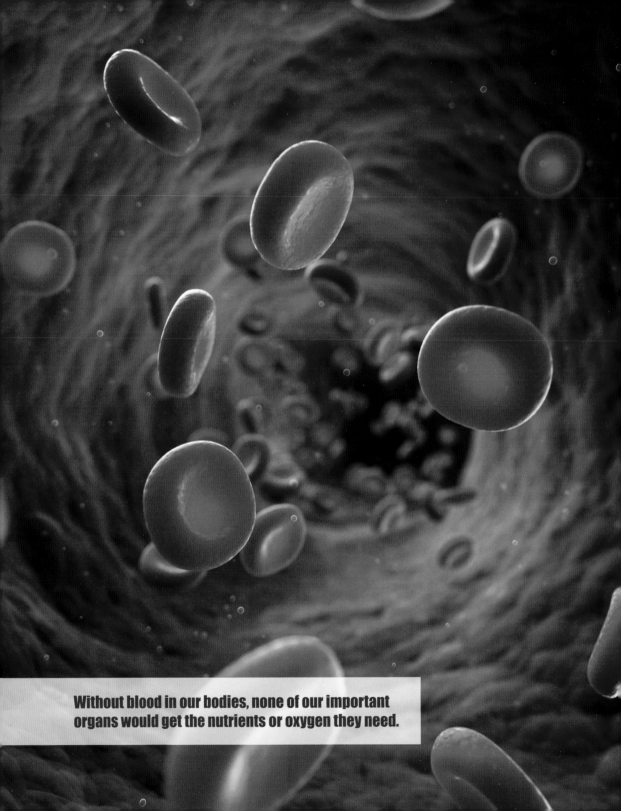

Without blood in our bodies, none of our important organs would get the nutrients or oxygen they need.

THE IMPORTANCE OF BLOOD

Blood is essential for life. Without it, oxygen and other nutrients couldn't reach the heart or every other cell in the body. It also carries waste products away. People can't live without blood. It helps keep us warm when it's cold, and it helps cool us off when it's hot.

How It's Made

Blood is made up of two parts: cells and a clear, yellowish liquid called plasma. The average adult has about 5.3 quarts (5 L) of blood. About 55 percent of that is plasma. About 90 percent of plasma is water. The other 10 percent is made up of waste products and substances we need for life. These include proteins—substances our bodies need to build, maintain, and replace tissues. They also include hormones, which are chemicals that affect the way our bodies function.

Fast Fact

Blood makes up 7 to 8 percent of a person's body weight.

Blood cells are made by **bone marrow**. In children, blood cells are made in the marrow of most bones. In adults, blood cells are produced in the marrow of the spine, breastbone, ribs, pelvis, upper arms, and upper legs.

There are two types of blood cells: red blood cells (RBCs) and white blood cells (WBCs). RBCs

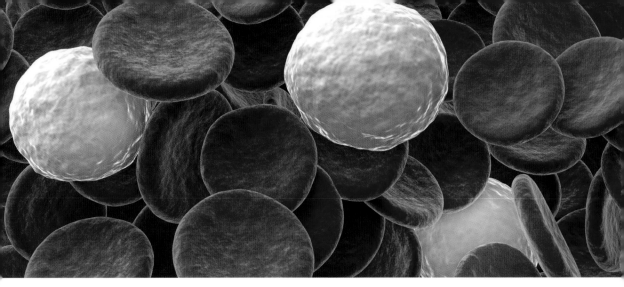

Red blood cells and white blood cells are important for helping our organs work.

carry oxygen from the lungs to the rest of the body. RBCs are round, flat disks with a biconcave shape. This means the surfaces on both sides of each cell curve inward. As blood passes through the lungs, oxygen attaches itself to a molecule in RBCs called hemoglobin. Hemoglobin is what makes blood appear red. Oxygen-poor blood is a darker red than oxygen-rich blood. RBCs wear out after about 120 days. They're replaced by new cells. Old RBCs are removed from the body by the **liver** and **spleen**.

Fast Fact

A blood transfusion is a process by which someone receives blood from another person. This often happens when someone has lost a lot of blood. Only certain blood types can be exchanged with one another.

Blood transfusions happen often during surgery.

What's Your Blood Type?

Blood comes in different "types." The different types are based on the presence or absence of proteins on the surface of RBCs. These proteins are called A and B. When someone is donating or receiving blood, it's very important for medical staff to know what type of blood that person has, or problems can occur.

Blood Type	Protein	Blood Donations
A	A	can be donated to As and ABs
B	B	can be donated to Bs and ABs
AB	both A and B	can be donated only to ABs
O	neither A nor B	can be donated to anyone

White blood cells help fight illnesses and infections in the body. An infection happens when germs enter the body and then increase in number. Germs are tiny things that make people sick and can only be seen under a microscope. The most common types of germs are bacteria. Some kinds of bacteria make people sick, while others are helpful. WBCs help fight "bad" bacteria and other germs that enter the body.

There are five major types of WBCs. Each has a different job. Some only go after a specific kind of germ. They surround the germs and "eat" them. Other WBCs use proteins called antibodies to attack germs. In people with allergies, WBCs overreact to normally harmless substances, such as dust, pollen, and mold, and think they're dangerous. Depending on the kind, WBCs live from a few days to a few weeks.

Clots, Scabs, and Scars

When blood vessels are damaged or cut, cell pieces called platelets rush to the injury. The platelets branch out and fit together like puzzle pieces to seal the wound. These tiny cell pieces use a protein to help them stick together. The clump that forms is called a clot. It forms a plug that keeps blood inside the vessels and germs outside. This is how we get scabs over cuts on the skin. Over time, the scab will fall off, and the skin will look like it was never injured. For deep wounds, sometimes a scar forms after the scab falls off. Scars are faint, visible marks on the skin. Sometimes, a scar will also be raised, or lifted. It's a reminder of the injury, but it doesn't hurt to touch or have on the skin.

Fast Fact

If you put pressure on an artery or nerve, a part of your body might lose blood flow temporarily. After you release the pressure, the body part might have a "pins and needles" feeling. That's the feeling of blood rushing back into the blocked area to restore circulation.

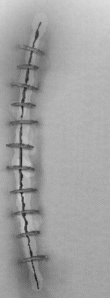
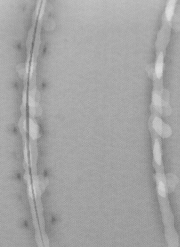

Shown here is what happens as a deep cut heals, leaving a scar.

RESPONDING TO FEAR

The "fight-or-flight response" is the human body's natural ability to prepare for a fight or run away. It's usually turned on when someone is faced with a frightful situation or one the brain thinks is frightful.

The brain first sends messages to several parts of the body. **Adrenaline** from the **adrenal glands** tells the heart to beat faster. It causes the arteries to grow narrower and the veins wider. This increases blood flow throughout the body, meaning the body will be able to perform more effectively. The **pituitary gland** releases endorphins—natural painkillers—into the bloodstream. People will likely feel a rush of energy in their body.

There have also been reports of people doing impossible-sounding things during a fight-or-flight state. Examples include lifting a car off of someone with one's bare hands or climbing quickly up a tree to get away from an animal.

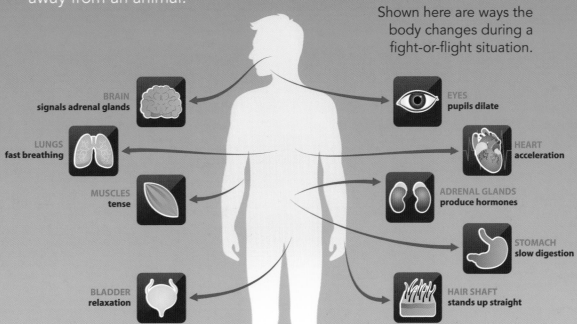

Shown here are ways the body changes during a fight-or-flight situation.

BRAIN
signals adrenal glands

LUNGS
fast breathing

MUSCLES
tense

BLADDER
relaxation

EYES
pupils dilate

HEART
acceleration

ADRENAL GLANDS
produce hormones

STOMACH
slow digestion

HAIR SHAFT
stands up straight

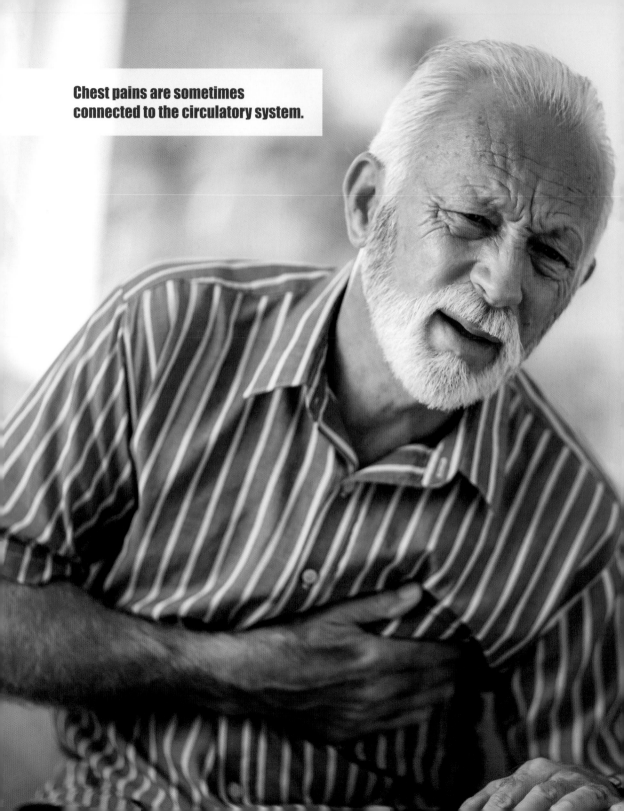

Chest pains are sometimes connected to the circulatory system.

PROBLEMS WITH THE CIRCULATORY SYSTEM

Sometimes, people get sick, and those sicknesses affect many parts of the body, including the circulatory system. Some diseases and disorders affect the heart and blood vessels, and some affect the blood.

Heart Disease

"Heart disease" is a general term for any disease that affects the blood vessels and heart. It's the number-one cause of death in the United States. The most common form is coronary artery disease. Fatty material builds up on artery walls, causing them to become narrow and "hardened." Blood flow to the heart is reduced. This can cause chest pain and a heart attack. A heart attack is a major medical emergency caused by the blockage of an artery to the heart. It can result in permanent heart damage or even death. Other common forms of heart disease include an uneven heartbeat and heart failure, which occurs when the heart can't pump enough blood throughout the body.

Fast Fact

According to the American Heart Association, almost half of the number of adults living in the United States have some sort of heart condition.

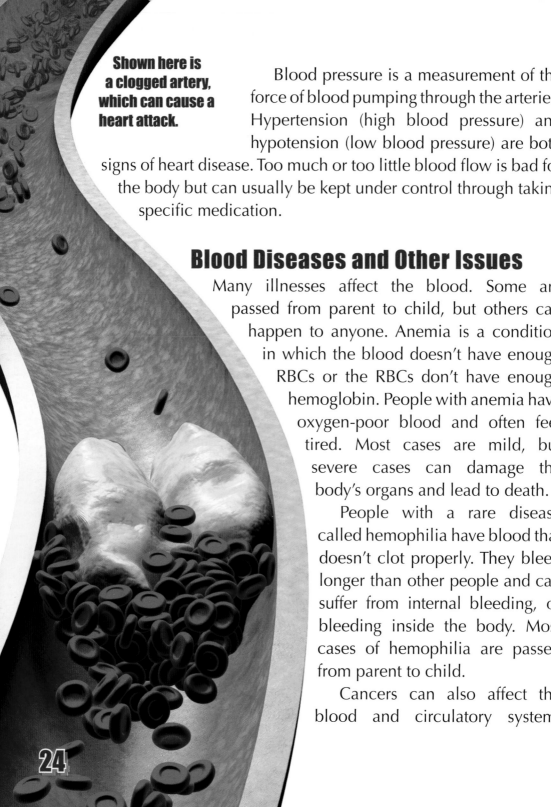

Shown here is a clogged artery, which can cause a heart attack.

Blood pressure is a measurement of the force of blood pumping through the arteries. Hypertension (high blood pressure) and hypotension (low blood pressure) are both signs of heart disease. Too much or too little blood flow is bad for the body but can usually be kept under control through taking specific medication.

Blood Diseases and Other Issues

Many illnesses affect the blood. Some are passed from parent to child, but others can happen to anyone. Anemia is a condition in which the blood doesn't have enough RBCs or the RBCs don't have enough hemoglobin. People with anemia have oxygen-poor blood and often feel tired. Most cases are mild, but severe cases can damage the body's organs and lead to death.

People with a rare disease called hemophilia have blood that doesn't clot properly. They bleed longer than other people and can suffer from internal bleeding, or bleeding inside the body. Most cases of hemophilia are passed from parent to child.

Cancers can also affect the blood and circulatory system.

COOL TECHNOLOGY: *STENTING*

Patients with coronary artery disease are benefiting from an amazing yet simple medical device. This device is called a stent, and it's being used in medical procedures related to the heart today.

A stent is a small wire-mesh or plastic tube designed to widen blocked arteries and restore normal blood flow to the heart. A tiny balloon is placed inside the stent. Doctors make a small cut in an arm or leg artery and then slide the stent along the artery to the blockage. The balloon is then filled with air, which causes the stent—as well as the artery—to open up. Then, the balloon is deflated, leaving the stent in place. Stents can stay inside the body permanently.

Shown here is a stent in action.

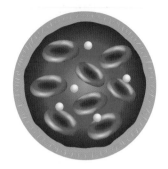
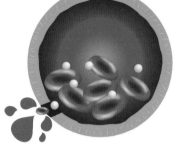
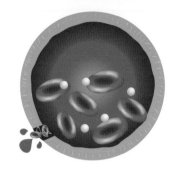

normal
blood vessel

bleeding starts

HEMOPHILIA
incomplete clot,
continued bleeding

Hemophilia is a disease that affects the blood.

Leukemia is a cancer that affects the bone marrow and blood. Bone marrow in people with leukemia produces a large number of WBCs that don't act like normal cells. In time, these abnormal WBCs crowd out healthy cells in the bloodstream, **lymph nodes**, liver, and spleen. Leukemia causes anemia, bleeding, and infections. Some forms of leukemia can be cured, some can be controlled, and others are deadly.

A pulmonary embolism is a sudden blockage in a lung artery. It's usually caused by a blood clot that travels from a vein in a leg to the lungs. It can be deadly if not treated immediately.

Have a Healthy Heart

What can you do to remain healthy and avoid diseases like these? The best advice for heart disease **prevention** is to keep your heart and the rest of

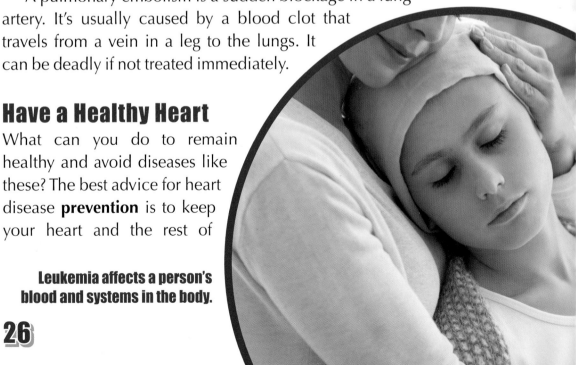

Leukemia affects a person's blood and systems in the body.

Eating well and exercising can help a person stay fit and have a healthy heart.

your body healthy. A regular exercise routine strengthens the circulatory system and improves blood flow. This helps the human body use oxygen better. Exercise also helps fight hypertension.

Eating too many fatty and sugary foods can lead to hypertension and coronary artery disease. Too much salt can also lead to hypertension. A diet high in fruits, vegetables, whole grains, and low-fat proteins will help keep your heart healthy. A healthy lifestyle helps keep the circulatory system running well!

Fast Fact

A drop of blood can have between 7,000 and 25,000 WBCs. Someone with leukemia might have 50,000 WBCs in a single drop of blood.

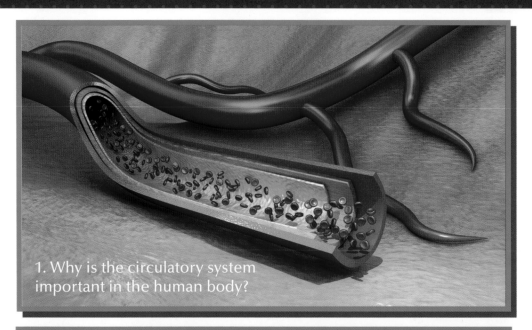

1. Why is the circulatory system important in the human body?

2. What type of circulatory system might a snail have? How is it different from a human's system?

3. How many chambers make up the heart? What are they called?

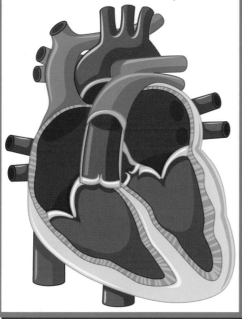

4. How can you keep your heart healthy?

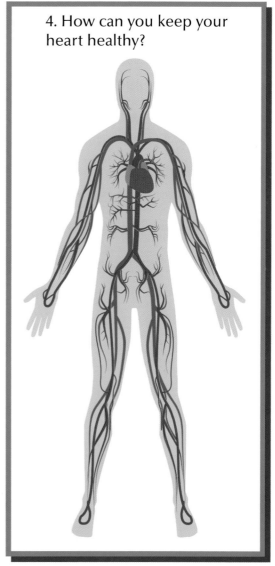

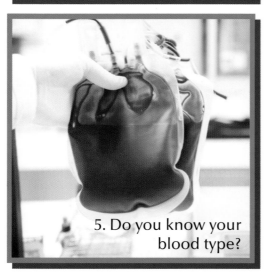

5. Do you know your blood type?

GLOSSARY

adrenal gland: A part of the body near the kidneys that lets out adrenaline when needed.

adrenaline: A chemical that creates a rush of energy in a person's body when something is frightening or exciting, giving them more strength.

blood vessel: A tube in the body that blood flows through as it transports oxygen, nutrients, and waste products around the body.

bone marrow: Soft matter inside bones where blood cells are made.

carbon dioxide: A waste substance produced by cells in the body when they create energy. It is given off by humans when we breathe out.

deoxygenated: Containing no oxygen.

diaphragm: A thin, curved muscle below the lungs.

extremity: A part of the body that is far away from the heart, such as a hand or foot.

liver: An organ that stores and cleans blood.

lymph node: A small body part that helps fight infection and diseases.

nerve: A string of cells that carries messages between the brain and other parts of the body.

nutrient: Something a living thing needs to grow and stay alive.

pituitary gland: Part of the body that controls horomones and other bodily functions.

prevention: Actions taken to stop something.

spleen: An organ that destroys old blood cells and stores blood.

FIND OUT MORE

Books

Gomdori Co. and Hyun-Dong Han. *Survive! Inside the Human Body, Vol. 2: The Circulatory System*. San Francisco, CA: No Starch Press, 2013.

Mason, Paul. *Your Hardworking Heart and Spectacular Circulatory System*. New York, NY: Crabtree Publishing, 2015.

Spilsbury, Richard, and Louise A. Spilsbury. *The Science of the Heart and Circulatory System*. New York: NY: Gareth Stevens Publishing, 2017.

Websites

American Heart Association
www.heart.org
Learn more about heart disease and how you can increase your chances of living a long, healthy life.

American Red Cross
www.redcross.org
Explore the mission of the Red Cross, a blood-donation organization, and learn how to get involved.

Your Heart and Circulatory System
kidshealth.org/kid/htbw/heart.html
Read more about the circulatory system.

INDEX